The Nehemiah Plan: Preparing the Church to Rebuild Broken Lives

Dr. Frank M. Reid, III

Treasure House

An Imprint of

Destiny Image

P.O. Box 310

Shippensburg, PA 17257

"For where your treasure is
there will your heart be also."Matthew 6:21

ISBN 1-56043-766-9

For Worldwide Distribution
Printed in the U.S.A.

Destiny Image books are available through these fine distributors outside the United States:

Christian Growth, Inc.
Jalan Kilang-Timor, Singapore 0315

Successful Christian Living
Capetown, Rep. of South Africa

Lifestream
Nottingham, England

Vision Resources
Ponsonby, Auckland, New Zealand

Rhema Ministries Trading
Randburg, South Africa

WA Buchanan Company
Geebung, Queensland, Australia

Salvation Book Centre
Petaling, Jaya, Malaysia

Word Alive
Niverville, Manitoba, Canada

Dedication

To my father, Bishop Frank Madison Reid, Jr., (1926-1989) who was my spiritual mentor and best friend.

To my daughter, "Joy" M. Reid, who died before we knew her, but not before we loved her.

Acknowledgments

Dr. Samuel DeWitt Proctor, Pastor Emeritus of the Abyssinia Baptist Church in Harlem, New York, has a very moving sermon entitled, "Taking Care of Unfinished Business". In the introduction (of the sermon), he reminds us that no matter how successful we become in life, somebody has nurtured us, taught us, encouraged us and aided us along the road of success. Those often unseen and forgotten people, Dr. Proctor points out, deserve to be acknowledged and thanked. To remember and recognize their contributions to our success is part of the unfinished business of life.

In structuring the contents of a book, the acknowledgments allow the author to remember those without whom the book would still be "unfinished business".

It is a humbling and helpful experience to attempt to remember those who helped make a God given dream a reality.

My entire family has been extremely helpful and supportive throughout his process. My mother, Adrenis Carter Reid, four sisters, Adrenise Veatrice Reid, Vanessa Reid Lewter, Stephanie Diane Reid, and Karla Francette Reid, have always encouraged me to reach for the stars.

The African Methodist Episcopal Church family provided me with the spiritual, educational and theological foundation upon which this book and my ministry have been built. Bishops Henry Wendell Murph, H. Hartford Brookins, and John Richard Bryant have been used by God to significantly shape my life and pastorate. Rev. William Donnell Watley and I grew up together in the A.M.E. Church. His example and gentle prodding are the main reasons this book is now finished.

The Bethel-Baltimore church family is the place where I am growing to new levels of spiritual maturity. The love and prayers of the officers, ministerial staff members and church organizations have made me a stronger and better pastor. It was in the Bethel pulpit that the first phase of this book was preached and taught. It was the many members of our television family, through their letters and phone calls, that made me see the need for this book.

Without friends, this book would have never gotten started. Dr. Kingsley Fletcher suggested Treasure House Press, Attorney Leronia Josey was irreplaceable in the first stages of the book's development, Betty Clark's support has been an ongoing inspiration, and Catherine Pugh gave helpful hints and plenty of her time to make sure that we finished with a quality product.

My editor Bob Buchannon, has done a Herculean job. His writing and editing skills have helped to make this a much stronger work. Helen Dale of Bethel-Baltimore also provided editorial insight and encouragement that was invaluable.

My wife, Marlaa, two daughters FranShon Marieé and Faith Mirachelle, the project managers, directed this work to fruition. In the midst of writing *The Nehemiah Plan*, we had a broken life experience when one of the twins my wife was carrying in her womb died in the eighth month of pregnancy. Since that time, she has worked on this project with great desire and determination. Without Marlaa's loving presence, hard work and commitment to be wife, mother and project manager, *The Nehemiah Plan* would have been just another good idea that remained unfinished.

Finally, to God be the glory for sending Jesus the Liberator and the Holy Ghost the Empowerer, to keep on rebuilding broken lives.

Contents

Introduction

Whether it is the latest mass suicide, or drug bust, the newspapers and daily television newscasts continually provide us with proof that we live in a broken world filled with broken people. We are regularly treated to a menu of dysfunctional and abusive behavior such as sexually abused children, young people who join gangs as a substitute for a supportive family structure, the spreading cancers of racism, sexism, and economic inequality. We recognize that these specific manifestations are symptoms of the brokenness of sin and rebellion against God.

The good news is that God has a plan for rebuilding for individuals and institutions that have experienced brokenness. The good news is that the purpose of the church is to bring healing and wholeness to a broken people and a broken generation.

Our churches are filled with people who are struggling with the consequences of broken hearts, broken families, broken relationships, broken dreams, broken spirits, and broken bodies. For many of them the church becomes a place to hide and lick their wounds. Meanwhile outside the church, the cycle of brokenness becomes stronger, more pervasive and more destructive.

The Old Testament book of Nehemiah, however, provides us with God's strategy for *rebuilding, restoring, reviving* and *resurrecting* His people.

The purpose of the Nehemiah plan is to move us from brokenness to boldness in God.

This new and authentic boldness manifests itself by helping broken people to become builders. The Nehemiah Plan shows us how God takes the broken pieces of humanity and transforms them into building blocks for His new creation. The Nehemiah Plan reminds us that out of the experience of brokenness God is going to build a new church, a new people, and a new generation that has His heart, His mind, His Spirit, His power and His joy!

The first stage in the rebuilding process is preparation. God prepared Nehemiah to become a rebuilder and Nehemiah prepared the people to take part in the rebuilding process. Today, God is preparing the church to take part in rebuilding broken lives, broken communities, broken nations, and a broken world.

Christians need to have an air of expectancy and excitement. God is about to do something wonderful, as His broken people become His building people. The obstacles that are placed in our way by the enemy can be overcome by our faithfulness to God. God is mighty. God is powerful. God will prevail.

As we look to Him for guidance, God's people can apply the principles of the ancient Biblical book of Nehemiah in an exciting new way. The opportunity to become builders and arise up out of the ashes of brokenness is upon God's church. Now is the time for us to prepare to rebuild!

Foreword

Behind every social problem, there is a spiritual solution!

The perplexing issues that people, nations, and governments are experiencing is evidence of global confusion. This dilemma can no longer be ignored. Everywhere you turn you see or hear of crime, corruption, sickness, disease, injustice, political and social unrest. It looks like society has a blatant disregard for human life.

Yet mankind longs for change. The change people need, first, is spiritual. God has provided all the answers we need. There are more answers than there are questions, although people prefer to only magnify questions and problems.

The social issues which face our world are merely symptoms of a greater problem. Lives which are void of spiritual commitment are more willing to accept social response to spiritual problems. Broken lives cannot be repaired by social programs alone.

The fundamental needs which must be met for one to know fulfillment in life are—Power, Authority, and Influence.

God is our power. Christ is our authority. The Holy Spirit is our influence. If we are to build or rebuild anything in our lives, God, Christ, and the Holy Spirit must be at the center of all we are, and will become. To do otherwise, would mean we choose to reject God's Nehemiah Plan.

This is an insightful book, *The Nehemiah Plan: Preparing the Church to Rebuild Broken Lives*. Dr. Frank M. Reid brilliantly presents his experience in addressing the issues and exploring the challenges facing us all. Ministers, lay persons, and leaders will understand Frank's succinct observation, "The purpose of God's Nehemiah Plan is to move us from brokenness to boldness in Him." Since our heritage is in the Lord, we must invest in our future.

Dr. Reid is a man of experience and depth, who is living the principles in this book. I am blessed by the powerful truths which my good friend and associate has presented. I highly recommend this book to anyone with an open mind and a desire for God's best.

May God richly bless you.

Dr. Kingsley Fletcher
Cary, North Carolina

Chapter 1

God's Plan for
a Broken World

Nehemiah 1:1.2 KJV

The words of Nehemiah the son of Hachaliah. And it came to pass in the month Chisleu, in the twentieth year, as I was in Shushan the palace, That Hanani, one of my brethren, came, he and certain men of Judah; and I asked them concerning the Jews that had escaped, which were left of the captivity, and concerning Jerusalem.

We live in a broken world that specializes in producing broken people. Children are born in our world. They are born in innocence and raised by adults in a world whose cultures and systems are hostile to innocence.

We live in a broken world that specializes in producing broken people. This lesson of brokenness is taught to children very early in their lives. In Western culture we teach children about brokenness by telling them a nursery rhyme.

Humpty Dumpty sat on the wall. Humpty Dumpty had a great fall. All the king's horses and all the king's men couldn't put Humpty together again.

The nursery rhyme attempts to teach children that brokenness is a reality of life. However, the ending is extremely painful. The ending teaches that when you are broken there is no power on earth that can put you back together again.

We live in a broken world that specializes in breaking people down. People and systems are breaking down all over the world. World events indicate that politically, economically and socially systems are breaking down. Everywhere we look, people and systems are breaking down.

A few years ago the Berlin Wall stood strong as the symbol of the hardness of the political system of East Germany, but now that Wall and that system has been broken down. A few years ago Russia was one of the major powers of the world. Today, the Soviet Union, as we once knew it, no longer exists. Even apartheid in South Africa, is slowly breaking down. We live in a world where political systems that seek to control, manipulate and govern the lives of people are constantly breaking down.

In America no matter how often our President says that we are out of the recession, as we look at the large numbers of people standing in lines to receive food, the figures of the unemployed and underemployed, we find that great America is going through a period of economic breakdown.

When one looks at the African American community in this nation, we find that our families are breaking down. Black men are being broken down by being sent either to prison or to an early grave. We find that the minds of our children are being broken down in an educational system that does not have enough money set aside to provide for their needs.

Everywhere we look, politically, economically, socially, and institutionally, we find brokenness. This brokenness is both institutional and individual. If we are honest with ourselves, there is brokenness inside each one of us: Broken dreams, broken hearts, broken aspirations, broken relationships, a broken sense of self esteem. Each one of us walks around with an inward brokenness that we have carried with us for so long that we don't even recognize that we are living out our pain and forcing our brokenness on other people.

And so the question that faces us today is "how are we going to deal with social or institutional brokenness?" We can deny it or we can turn it over to the Lord. We have the power to choose. We can acknowledge or deny our brokenness. Will you deny it or deal with it? God says to all of His people that there is but one way to deal with your brokenness. God wants to help you rebuild the broken places in your life.

God provides us with the Nehemiah Plan so that we might rebuild whatever the broken places are in our communities and in our individual lives.

Just because you are broken doesn't mean you must stay broken. Just because you are defeated, doesn't mean you must stay defeated. Just because you are negative, does not mean you have to stay negative. God has a plan for your life and for my life that will allow us to take the broken places and rebuild them through the power of Almighty God.

The ancient book of Nehemiah provides relevant guidance for rebuilding. It is a book about rebuilding an ancient city that was broken, ruined and filled with broken people. Yet, God called and used Nehemiah to rebuild out of the brokenness.

Nehemiah 1:1-3

> *The words of Nehemiah son of Hacaliah: In the month of Kislev in the twentieth year, while I was in the citadel of Susa, Hanani, one of my brothers came from Judah with some other men, and I questioned them about the Jewish remnant that survived the exile, and also about Jerusalem. They said to me, "Those who survived the exile and are back in the province are in great trouble and disgrace. The wall of Jerusalem is broken down, and its gates have been burned with fire."*

Nehemiah was a middle class autocrat who had a comfortable lifestyle working for the oppressor of his people. Nehemiah was a part of a people who, because of their rebelliousness against God, had their community and religious heritage broken.

God had separated the Jews for His purposes hundreds of years before. He called Abraham, promised to bless him and his descendants, and made him into a great nation. They were slaves in Egypt, but God delivered them from slavery through the leadership of Moses.

Moses led the people through the wilderness. Joshua led them into the promised land. Here they were to enjoy a land of blessing, flowing with milk and honey. However, they forgot about God and continually sought foreign ways and pagan gods.

The Jewish people had been a great empire under the direction of King David. Within only two generations they were a nation divided by civil war and strife due to their continual backsliding and selfishness. It was because of unfaithfulness that they were divided into two nations. Finally, God allowed them to be conquered by another empire due to their sins. First, the northern nation fell, and finally the southern nation and Jerusalem fell.

When Jerusalem was captured, the Jewish people were taken captive. Any of those who had merit were led to Babylon where they became slaves. The decades of captivity were a miserable time for Jews. However, their suffering caused them to call out to God for relief. Once again, God restored them. He softened the heart of the emperor and allowed them to return to Jerusalem and Judah.

A great prophet, Ezra, returned to Jerusalem to rebuild the Temple of God. He was a religious man who once again, taught the people the Word of God.

There was a great revival in the land. However, they needed more. The people were wounded and broken by their heritage and history of captivity. They needed someone to help them rebuild the city that was broken. The city was the symbol of their faith and strength. It had to be restored.

One hundred years had passed since the people were allowed to return to Jerusalem. They were free, yet they were broken. They had rights and privileges, yet they remained in poverty. God was burdening the heart of another great leader so that they could find restoration.

Nehemiah was a trusted confidant of the Persian King Artaxerxes, the cup bearer of the king. This was a position of great power and authority. Many of those who had been made slaves in Babylon became powerful figures in that empire, as well as the empire of the Medes and Persian followers.

Some records indicate that the cup bearer was often a special advisor to the king who had the royal signet through which he could make laws and decrees. Nehemiah was selected by God to be in the right place at the right time in order to restore His people at Jerusalem and the holy city.

Nehemiah was visited by one of his brothers, Hanani, and another group of men who came from Judah. He asked about the condition of his people and city. Nehemiah told Hanani about the conditions of his less fortunate brothers and sisters. Even though Nehemiah had the material wealth and position that would allow him to be classified as successful, he was concerned about the religious heritage and restoration of his people.

As we look closely at the first, second, and third verses, we find those principles that are prerequisite to us for rebuilding the broken places in our community and our lives.

I. Concern

If we are to begin the process of rebuilding, we must be concerned. How sad it is that we live in a world that is filled with lack of concern and apathy. Folks are often not concerned about anything or anybody but their own self-satisfaction. The reason why you and I have what we have today is because there was somebody in our lives who prayed for us and sacrificed that we might enjoy the benefits of their sacrifice.

When the civil rights struggle was taking place in this country, those men and women marched and suffered and died, not just so they could get something for themselves, but because they were concerned for generations that were yet unborn. Now we have raised a generation filled with people that are so self-centered and selfish that they are not concerned about anybody or anything but themselves. When you are selfish and self-centered and have no concern about anybody but yourself, there is a spiritual cancer on the inside that could destroy our community.

The boys and girls that commit crime and use dope do so because of teachers and churches that are not concerned. When doctors and lawyers that used to live in the black community move out and forget where they came from, they have lost their concern.

If we are to begin to rebuild, we must recapture this sense of concern for ourselves and for others that Nehemiah had for his people.

II. Compassion

If we are going to rebuild we must also have the same kind of compassion as Nehemiah. We must recover that sense of compassion for ourselves, our communities, cities and nation. How easy it would have been for Nehemiah to enjoy his middle class lifestyle. How easy it would have been for him to turn his back on his hurting and homeless brothers and sisters. What Nehemiah knew was that had it not been for the compassion of Almighty God he would not have been as fortunate. If God's compassion blesses us, it is not because we are so smart, or good looking, it is because of the gracious compassion of Almighty God.

When we have received compassion then we have a responsibility to show compassion to others. Isn't it something that years ago in our community, we did not have to worry about what would happen to children whose parents died. It was because there was some-body, either in the family or in the neighborhood, who may not have a lot of money, but they had com-passion, and were willing to share their blessing to make sure those children had a roof over their head, clothes on their backs and were educated. This is the kind of compassion that allowed us to save genera-tions of youth from destruction. It is this same sense of compassion that is needed today, for us to save the generation we are losing and for us to rebuild the brokenness that exists in our lives.

III. Consciousness

Nehemiah understood that individualism by it-self can destroy a people and a community. He was conscious of the conditions of his brothers and sis-ters. He was also conscious about the condition of his religious heritage. He had been taught that it is necessary to have a God-consciousness, and that God-consciousness develops a high sense of self-esteem.

Nehemiah's God-consciousness gave him love for himself, his religion and his people. When we are without God-consciousness we can hate ourselves and those who look like us. Many of us will change our names to reflect other religions or cultures and because we do not have a God-consciousness, even with these new names, whether they be African or Arabic, some of us are still guilty of selling dope and killing our children.

If we are going to rebuild, we must recover our God-consciousness. When you recover your God-consciousness, you will understand that all of us are important in God's eyes because he made us. When you recover your God-consciousness, you will understand that God does not make junk. No matter what color your skin or how dark or light it is, God does not make junk. No matter how short and curly or long and straight your hair, God does not make junk. Whether you live in the projects or live in a penthouse, God does not make junk. Whether you have a college education or no education, God does not make junk. If you are a single parent, you are not by yourself, God does not make junk. When you know who you are, you know you belong to God. You have developed a God Consciousness and understand God will be your way-maker, your burden bearer, and your bridge over troubled water.

IV. Change

When you recover your concern, your compassion and God-consciousness, God will give you the power to change your life and the lives of those around you.

What we need today is change. We need black men who are willing to say, "I don't have to stay on alcohol. I don't have to commit crimes to make it. I don't have to beat my woman and abuse my children. I'm going to change." We need middle class folk who are willing to say, "If I have to drive from the suburbs to the ghetto, I'm going to help somebody because it is time for a change." We need churches that are willing to use their resources not just to build new buildings, but to build new lives.

I was reading a book that was recommended highly entitled *Wake Up America* by Tony Campolo. He tells a true story of a young man in Philadelphia who came from Korea and graduated from Eastern College, a Christian college. He went on to get an advanced degree from the University of Pennsylvania. One day he went to mail a letter at the post office. While he was walking, he was accosted by a group of young thugs; young men for whom the world and the political system had no compassion.

They were young, broken, men who robbed and stole to make a living. The young thugs became angry because the victim didn't have a lot of money and they beat him to death. The crime was outrageous. The Philadelphia police arrested them and their trial received a great deal of media attention.

The victim's family flew from Korea for the trial. At the end of the trial, when the murderers were found guilty, but prior to the judge passing his sentence, the parents asked if they could say a word. They got down on their knees in the courtroom in front of the judge and asked him to give them the boys that killed their son. They were Christians and they wanted to take these boys back to Korea and provide for them the concern, compassion and God-consciousness that was needed to change these young men's lives. The judge denied the parents request. He explained to them that our judicial system doesn't work that way. This judge did not have the power to rebuild broken lives. Like all the king's men in the nursery rhyme Humpty Dumpty, the judge could not put the broken lives of the Korean parents or the young African-American men "back together again."

The nursery rhyme Humpty Dumpty ends negatively and destructively. It says, "all the kings horses and all the kings men couldn't put Humpty Dumpty together again." Today, we find that all the political, economic and sociological strategies have not been able to put our broken world and the people in it back together again.

Years after I had become an adult, I began to wonder why the broken Humpty Dumpty was left in the hands of the Kings men? Why didn't they take this brokenness directly to the King? Those of us who have experienced God's concern, compassion, commitment know how our broken lives have been changed and are clear that God has a plan for our broken world. That plan is to bring broken people, broken families and broken systems to The King! King Jesus! For Jesus does have the power to take our broken lives, our broken world and put them together again.

Humpty Dumpty sat on the wall.
Humpty Dumpty had a great fall.
All the kings horses and all the king's men
took him to King Jesus and He put Humpty Dumpty
together again.

Finally in the words of one of the great Christian hymns:

It is no secret what God can do.
What He's done for others, He'll do for you.
With arms wide open, He'll pardon you.
It is no secret what God can Do.

Review and Application

1. How did God prepare Nehemiah for leadership?

2. How does rebuilding the community truly begin within each of us?

3. How does individualism, by itself, contribute to the decline of the community?

4. What is the source of our ability to change?

Chapter 2

Strength to Rebuild

Nehemiah 2:18 KJV

Then I told them of the hand of my God which was good upon me; as also the king's words that he had spoken unto me. And they said, Let us rise up and build. So they strengthened their hands for this good work.

We find in the book of Nehemiah that the love of God enables and empowers us to rebuild the broken places that hinder us from being all that we can be. A broken heart can hold us back from taking part in an authentic and loving relationship. Broken self-esteem can stop us from exemplifying a positive and productive personality. A broken spirit finds it virtually impossible to experience real joy. Brokenness leads to weakness. These weaknesses often serve as the road blocks to our becoming all that the Lord created us to be and achieve. We need the love of God to teach us how to rebuild the broken places. God provides for each of us, for each church, each city, each state, each nation and each family a plan by which we can rebuild the broken places in our lives. We may suffer from broken hearts, broken relationships and broken dreams, but God has provided principles in the ancient text of Nehemiah to help us find success. For after we receive God's plan to rebuild our broken world, next we have to seek and receive the strength to rebuild.

Nehemiah challenged the people by explaining that he had been sent from the king with the power to rebuild the city of Jerusalem. The people had the faith and hope to respond by committing to the task.

Nehemiah 2:18 KJV

Then I told them of the hand of my God which was good upon me; as also the king's words that he had spoken unto me. And they said, Let us rise up and build. So they strengthened their hands for this good work.

We must have strength to rebuild the broken places that exist inside America. In spite of all the rhetoric we hear, America has become a weak nation. We find our nation too weak to deal with and overcome the oppressive problems of racism. From the Rodney King beating and the mishandling of his first case to the supreme Court ruling in 1993 that started to roll back the positive political consequences of the Voting Rights Act of the 1960's, America has proven itself to be too weak to handle the real problem of racism in this land.

America has become a weak nation. We find, no matter what the President wants to say, that the economic strategy of our government has continued to weaken our nation, to the point that the debt is now in the trillions of dollars. That debt continues to sap the economic strength of our nation. America is a weak nation. America is weak politically, morally and economically. America is falling apart because it is too weak to formulate a plan that can rebuild the broken places in this nation.

Those of us who are members of other racial and ethnic groups can take no pride in the weakness of America. The weakness of this nation has also invaded our lives, our families and our communities. There was a time when African Americans were a strong people. We did not have a lot of material things, but we had a lot of inner strength.

Strong mothers had something on the inside that made them stable and enabled them to raise their children in spite of all the pressures that they had to endure. There was a time when African American men were strong men; when we would not allow certain things to happen in our community, when we would not allow our women to be disrespected, when we would not allow crime to run rampant in our neighborhood. We were the policemen of our home and our communities. We built and supported our institutions, schools, colleges, hospitals, fraternal organizations, newspapers, and insurance companies.

We were strong women and strong men that produced strong children who were able to look and deal with racism and produce a Rosa Parks, a Paul Robeson, and a Dr. Charles Drew. We were a strong people in the midst of very intense trials and tribulations. In slavery, we produced men and women like

Rev. Nat Turner, Methodist class leader Denmark Vesey, Sojourner Truth, Harriet Tubman, Rev. Henry Highland Garnett, who strongly resisted the ungodly institution of American slavery. After the positive programs of American Reconstruction were rolled back and Jim Crowism and "separate but equal" ruled the land, we refused to succumb to weakness and produced strong institutions like The NAACP and strong individuals like Ida Wells Barnett, W.E.B. Dubois, Booker T. Washington and Marcus Garvey to sustain us in the midst of our brokenness. Today we find that, not only do we live in a weak nation, we also find that we have become a weak people. Instead of adults being in charge of children, now our children are in charge of us. Our children take control of many classrooms. Some of our children have instilled fear in our community. We talk about these problems, but find ourselves too weak to deal with them.

Many of our public schools have become armed camps where teachers and students are afraid that violence will break out any minute. Children are getting involved in criminal and violent behavior at an earlier age. The teen-age pregnancy rate continues to grow at epidemic proportions. We talk about these problems but find ourselves too weak to deal with them. We want our children to come to church. We want them to know about God, but we are too weak to instill in them the spiritual foundation that we know they need.

Many of us give our children things, like cars, clothes, and compact disc players. We given them things instead of time and understanding. Things are no substitute for strength. So we are a weak people living in a weak nation and no matter how expensive the clothes we wear, no matter how many Malcolm X T-shirts we put on, these things are no more than an Afro-centric attempt to cover-up the weakness that resides inside of us. We are a weak people living in the midst of a weak nation.

If you are like me, you have struggled with some weakness. Everyone has tried to break a habit. Each of us has tried to change some aspect of our lives. We have started out with the best of intentions and then found we were too weak. We did not have the strength to break that negative relationship. We did not have the strength to stop smoking those cigarettes. We did not have the strength to stop taking part in abusive behavior. We often find ourselves falling deeper and deeper into the abyss of weakness.

We take great stock in all the black mayors and other black politicians we've elected. We boast about all of the millionaires we have as a people. All of that cannot hide the fact that we are still weak. Too many of our young men go to early graves and too many of our young teenage women are still having babies out of wedlock. Too many of our older people are committing suicide because they believe that nobody loves them. In the face of this reality, we are tragically weak.

If we look closely at the Book of Nehemiah, we find that the Jews also were a weak people. They were a people whom God had brought back from the land to which they had been put into slavery. Even when they were returned to their land, they were too weak to rebuild that which had been broken down.

Have you tried to rebuild some of the broken places in your own life? Have you been a part of an organization that wanted to rebuild the black family and restore the black child? Did you find, however, that with all of that wonderful desire and purpose that somehow you still could not find the strength to rebuild?

The question that faces us today as Christians, as a Christian church, as a people, and as a nation is "How can we find the strength to rebuild the broken places?" We know they are broken. We know they need to be rebuilt. Somehow we cannot find the strength and discipline to rebuild our own lives and then to rebuild our communities.

When we look at the 18th verse of the second chapter of Nehemiah, we find that we are given some principles that will teach us how to find the strength to rebuild. The first point is that Nehemiah gave the people a vision. There can be no rebuilding going on unless God gives the vision. Nehemiah shared God's vision for the rebuilding of the community.

Unless God provides the vision, no rebuilding can take place. No matter how wonderful the plan the politicians and civil rights leaders put together, unless it comes from Almighty God, there will be no rebuilding.

When Nehemiah shared the vision with the people, the people that were weak caught the vision. We have got to catch God's vision for our life and for our community. I will remind all of our politicians, and all of those who want the best for America, that the civil rights movement did not start as a political movement; it started as a religious movement that came out of the Church of God. Until we go back to church, not just to say that we belong to church, but until our leaders come back to church and say, "It's me Lord standing in the need of prayer," they will continue to be blown by the winds of every political doctrine that comes by. The vision for rebuilding our community and our lives must come from God. For where there is no vision, the people perish.

I. Repentance

When the people caught the vision, the people said, "Let us rise up and rebuild." They got excited because they knew that God was on their side. When you know that God is on your side, no matter how broken you are, no matter what you have done, it makes you want to shout. It gives you joy in the midst of sorrow. It gives you gladness in the midst of sadness. They said, "Let us rise up and rebuild."

Like most other things in life, it's not just enough to say it. We have got to do something about it. The people of God were challenged enough by Nehemiah's proclamation that they began to gain strength to do the task. They allowed strength to be built up in their hands. They sensed a confidence that they would indeed see the city restored.

How did they strengthen their hands? They repented. We cannot receive strength to rebuild the broken places until we repent before God for our sins. It was sin that broke down the walls in the first place. Real repentance is not simply saying we are sorry, it requires a change of attitude and action.

If you are having problems with your children, don't start by totally blaming your children, repent of the parental mistakes you have made. If you are having problems in your marriage, don't blame it all on your husband or wife, repent for your part in making your marriage weak. If you want the community to be a better place, don't always point the finger at somebody, repent for what you have not done—for the times you have not voted, for the times you didn't give money to a black institution. We have got to repent.

Repentance! That is where we are weakest. Human pride that keeps us from repenting also keeps us from attaining the blessings God has in store for us. Repentance unlocks the blessing of God in our lives and strengthens us. Restoration will only come through our faithful repentance.

David, king of Israel, was at the apex of his power. He had conquered all of his enemies. He was wealthy and affluent. He had accomplished tasks that no one in the land had seen accomplished. Yet, in all of his power and strength, his failure to repent brought devastation.

One day, while his troops were off fighting a war, he was relaxing on the roof of his palace. While he was there he looked with interest at a neighboring house. He saw a pretty woman by the name of Bathsheba. She was married to one of his most loyal soldiers by the name of Uriah. King David wanted what somebody else had.

He desired this woman passionately. He was the king. He took it upon himself to take this woman from Uriah. He brought Bathsheba to the palace and had sexual relations with her. He enjoyed her immensely, but his ecstasy was interrupted when he realized that she had become pregnant because of his adultery.

In order to cover up his sin, David had Uriah brought home from the war. He thought everyone would think that Uriah had slept with his wife when she became pregnant. However, Uriah was an extremely honorable man. He refused to enjoy the company of his wife when his comrades were fighting at the front. He slept outside the king's palace.

David's plan was thwarted. Everyone would know that he and Bathsheba were having an affair. He stooped to murder to cover up his sin. He had Uriah moved to the front of the battle line, and secretly ordered everyone else to retreat. Uriah was left alone and defenseless. He was killed by the enemy, but it was actually the desire of the king that took his life.

God revealed David's sin to a prophet. He came to King David and confronted him by telling a hypothetical story. David became angry because of the supposed sin of Nathan's imaginary character, that he actually condemned himself with his own words.

No doubt David was a wretched man because of what he did. Certainly he deserved to die because of his passion and murder. However, God knew David's heart. David repented. God always honors repentance.

He lied and murdered to get what he wanted. His repentance is reflected in a song that he wrote during the ordeal. It stands as a testimony of the power of repentance to this day.

Psalm 51:1-13

Have mercy on me, O God, according to your unfailing love, according to your great compassion blot out my transgressions. Wash away all my iniquity and cleanse me from my sin. For I know my transgressions, and my sin is always before me. Against you, you only, have I sinned and done what is evil in your sight, so that you are proved right when you speak and justified when you judge. Surely I was sinful at birth, sinful from the time my mother conceived me. Surely you desire truth in the inner parts; you teach me wisdom in the inmost place. Cleanse me with hyssop, and I will be clean; wash me, and I will be cleaner than snow. Let me hear joy and gladness; let the bones you have crushed rejoice. Hide your face from my sins and blot out all my iniquity. Create in me a pure heart, O God, and renew a steadfast spirit within me. Do not cast me from your presence or take your Holy Spirit from me Restore to me the joy of your salvation and grant me a willing spirit, to sustain me. Then I will teach transgressors your ways, and sinners will turn back to you.

David repented before God and asked for a clean heart, He wanted his spirit to be steadfast and right. He also sang a prayer for joy to be restored to him. He prayed for the joy of salvation to return.

You can have position and not have joy. You can have money and cars, and not have joy. You can live in a fine house with all your degrees and not have joy. Like David, we need to cry out, "Lord, we repent! Restore unto us the joy of our salvation!"

II. Resources

If we are going to strengthen our hands, we have got to repent. Not only must we repent, we also have to organize our resources. The people of Jerusalem responded to Nehemiah by saying, "Let us rise up and rebuild" and they strengthened their hands. That means they began to organize their resources.

We, as a people, need to organize our resources for the rebuilding of the Kingdom. I could talk about economic development, but there will never be an economic development until there is first spiritual development.

We need to develop the resource of reading God's Word. You will have no strength unless you read and study God's Word. Your neighbor will have no strength unless they read and study God's Word. That is why so many believers are weak. We may bring the Bible to church, but all too often we put it back down when we get home and fail to absorb the Word at home.

There is power in the Word of God. God's Word says the Lord is my light and salvation. Whom shall I fear, for the Lord is the strength of my life of whom shall I be afraid (Ps. 27:1-2). There is power in the Word of God. There is strength in the Word of God.

God's Word is a resource. Not only must we organize our resources through the reading of God's Word, we have to organize our resources through prayer. Praying people are strong people. Those who pray do not walk in their own strength, they walk in the strength of God.

We need to stop praying only when we have problems. If you pray in good times and bad times, God will give you the strength to bear every problem and to bear every burden. There is power in prayer. There is strength in prayer.

We also have to organize our resources through faith. We have lost faith in ourselves. We don't have faith in ourselves as people any longer. You can't have faith in yourself if you don't have faith in God. The burden is lifted when we walk by faith and not by sight.

The people of Nehemiah's day organized their resources. They restored themselves to the Lord through the Word, prayer, and faith. However, God has a miraculous way of intervening on our behalf.

The next resource is of the Holy Spirit. The Holy Spirit doesn't just make you shout. The Holy Spirit makes you live right. The Holy Spirit is power. The Holy Spirit does not give us power to be spiritual entertainers that put on spiritual makeup on Sunday and act like something we are not. The Holy

Spirit does not help us become hypocrites. When the Holy Spirit is moving in your life, He gives you power to stand up to evil. He gives you power to raise your children. He gives you power to stand when all around you is falling.

III. Revival

When the people repented and organized their resources, then a revival broke out. Revival broke out and the broken places were rebuilt. Revival broke out and the weak became strong. Revival broke out and those individuals and institutions that were spiritually dead received new life. We need a revival in America. We need a revival in Black America. A revival is not something that just happens in the church. A revival is something that happens on inner city streets. A revival is something that happens in the worst projects of our land. When people have received the vision from God and begin to organize the resources that they do have, then they cry out, "Let us rise up and rebuild." That's Revival!

If Christians would take the light of God into the worst of America's neighborhoods, some little boy or little girl would stand up and say, "Let us rise up and rebuild." If we go to the dope dealers and tell them the wages of sin is death, but the gift of God is eternal life, some dope addicts would cry out, "Let us rise and rebuild." If middle class evil church folk would stop wearing their religion on their back and put it on their feet, and let God come into their heart, they would rise and say, "Let us stand up and rebuild." That's Revival!

You can have a full church and that church be full of empty people. Jesus did more with 12 disciples than many churches with thousands of members can accomplish. This was in spite or the fact that one of His disciples was a traitor. He had only eleven who were faithful. Jesus organized and refined their spiritual resources to strengthen the disciples for the task of rebuilding broken lives. That's Revival!

If every medical technician and doctor organized their spiritual resources, we could provide health care for the poor. If every lawyer would break out of an attitude of fear of lawsuits and organize their legal talent, we could provide free legal services to those who were in need. That's revival!

When you take one step towards God. God takes two steps towards you. If our teachers and public school administrators sat down and said, "We are going to come up with an educational plan for the children of our church and neighborhood," then they would find that a transformation would take place in the children who go to class. That's Revival! You cannot take a child out of a community where hate and division is taught and not expect them to be hateful and cantankerous. If you provide for them a community filled with love and care, it would make all the difference in the world. How can a child see compassion as legitimate if those who espouse compassion are simply following their employment contract.

Today, God is calling all of us to participate in a revival that rebuilds and strengthens broken lives and communities. God is challenging us to awaken from our slumber and take a long hard look at what is going on around us. The Prodigal son woke up in a pig pen. He opened his eyes and saw that his own selfishness had landed him in filth. When he took a good look at his condition he changed his direction, returned to his Father and revival took place. He gathered his resources and went back to his father.

The people of Jerusalem had been set free from slavery. They were struggling to survive. The city was in ruins and the walls were broken down. However, it took a man of God to come and wake them up to their condition. When you walk through the same neighborhood every day, you can begin to think that the brokenness around you is normal. Some give up and decide that the walls can simply stay broken down. Others are hopeless and miserable, because they have come to see brokenness as the only way to live. They allow broken surroundings to keep them weak.

When Nehemiah surveyed the condition of Jerusalem he reported to the people that there is a better way. There is hope for the city. It does not have to be destitute and in ruins. The wall can be built up once again. Strength to rebuild is available. Revival can take place.

Nehemiah had a vision from God. God paved the way for Nehemiah to come to Jerusalem. God gave Nehemiah the resources of King Artaxerxes to rebuild. In spite of all that Nehemiah had, he still needed the people. He could not rebuild the city alone. In spite of government intervention, the city could not be restored without the people taking part in God's plan. The people had to be revived and strengthened if broken lives and a broken community was going to be rebuilt.

It takes the strength of the people to restore and rebuild a city. Strength comes from recognizing sin and repenting, so that revival can begin. It is time for the cities of America to come to their knees and repent, so that revival can break out in the land.

Finally, it is exciting to know that no matter how weak we are; no matter how broken we are; God will provide us with strength to rebuild our broken lives and communities.

If we are willing to repent and participate in organizing our resources God will send us Holy Ghost power that will strengthen us for the work of rebuilding and revival.

The cities of America need people that are willing to recognize God's power and be changed. Our cities need people who have hope and purpose. That hope comes through the powerful life that Christ offers.

2 Corinthians 5:17-20

Therefore, if anyone is in Christ, he is a new creation; the old has gone, the new has come! All this is from God, who reconciled us to Himself through Christ and gave us the ministry of reconciliation: that God was reconciling the world to Himself in Christ, not counting men's sins against them. And He has committed to us the message of reconciliation. We are therefore Christ's ambassadors, as though God were making His appeal through us. We implore you on Christ's behalf: Be reconciled to God.

The revived and rebuilt lives of believers have the capacity and potential to revitalize and restore the city. There can be no doubt that God, giving hope to His people, will work through them to bring restoration. God's people are to be the leaders in the struggle to rebuild. They are to be the ambassadors who bring Christ's message of love and justice to those who need it most.

As in Nehemiah's time, the people must begin to strengthen themselves through developing resources for change. Spiritual resources, made possible by repentance, will provide the strength of character and with that we can revive the cities of our world.

Review and Application

1. Do you agree that America is a weak nation, why?

2. What is our source of vision?

3. How did the people strengthen themselves after hearing the vision?

4. What resources are available for us to rebuild?

Chapter 3

We Will Rise Up

Nehemiah 2:19-20 KJV

*But when Sanballat the Horonite, and Tobiah
the servant, the Ammonite, and Geshem the
Arabian, heard it, they laughed us to scorn,
and despised us and said, What is this thing
that ye do? will ye rebel against the king? Then
answered I them, and said unto them, The God
of heaven, He will prosper us; therefore we His
servants will arise and build: but ye have no
portion, nor right, nor memorial in Jerusalem.*

nyone who takes the time to study how oppressors stay in power will find that one of the major tools in the arsenal of any oppressor is discouragement. You may remember Alex Haley's movie and book "Roots." There is a very moving scene where the young Kunta Kinte, who has run away from slavery many times, only to be recaptured, refuses to be called by his slave name, Toby.

After having been caught again, young Kunta is tied to a tree and beaten unmercifully. Every time the pain becomes too heavy for him to bear, they pour water on him or grind salt into his wounds to bring him back to consciousness. The slave master asked, "What's your name, boy?" He said, "My name is Kunta." Again he receives an unmerciful beating.

In this incident, they did not beat Kunta (Toby) in isolation, they made all of the slaves watch. They beat and beat him until finally he said, "My name is Toby." The movie did an excellent job of letting us feel the depressed spirits of the people, and how discouraged they became when he finally said Toby.

One of the major tools in the arsenal of any oppressor is the tool of discouragement. If the oppressor can discourage you from rising up, he doesn't need guns, he doesn't need armies, and he doesn't need to use the power of force. He can simply discourage you from even trying to stand up and rebuild.

Discouragement is one of the major tools in the arsenal of every oppressor. When one looks closely at the second chapter of the book of Nehemiah, we find that in the eighteenth verse, after having shared God's vision with the people, that the people of God respond to Nehemiah's vision by saying, "Let us rise up and build."

Nehemiah 2:19-20 KJV

> *But when Sanballat the Horonite and Tobiah, the servant, the Ammonite, and Geshem the Arabian heard it, they laughed us to scorn and despised us and said, what is this thing that ye do? Will ye rebel against the king? Then answered I them and said unto them, The God of heaven, He will prosper us; Therefore, we His servants will arise and build. But ye have no portion, no right, nor memorial in Jerusalem.*

The people were excited and energized because they finally saw a plan that would release them from their oppression. As soon as the people began to organize to rebuild, we find that the opposition began to laugh, scorn, and despise them, asking, "What is this thing that ye do? Will ye rebel against the king?"

It was the king who sent Nehemiah back to Jerusalem in the first place. What the opposition was trying to do was to discourage them from rising up and building.

If you and I are going to rebuild the broken places in our lives, if you and I are going to rebuild the broken communities in which we live; if we are going to reclaim the broken people who are in prison and homeless and hungry and are substance abusers and sit in our congregations on a daily basis: we must know how to deal with discouragement.

The reason we are not dealing with our problems is because discouragement has paralyzed many of us. While we may know that the problem is discouragement, it still paralyzes us. While we know the broken areas in our lives and in our community, discouragement stops us from doing what we can to rebuild the broken places. The question that faces us as Christians, and as people living in this broken nation is, How do we rise up and build in the midst of this discouragement?

How in the midst of a public school system that has proven that they are not able to educate young African-American men and women, will we rise up and train these young people so that they will be able to live and succeed in an information society?

What is also discouraging today is that no matter how much progress we have made materially, the relationship between the African American man and African American woman is still less than what God would have it to be. We fail to address it because we are discouraged at being able to overcome this very major problem in our midst. Further we find that people in all ethnic groups have become so discouraged that many of us have given over to allowing oppression to exist in the political and economic system of our land. In a society that is filled with discouragement, discouraged people ultimately look for an outlet for their discouragement.

One outlet for discouragement is addiction. The reason that we are an addictive culture is that we have lived in discouragement for so long. We are addicted not only to drugs and alcohol, but to television. We have also become addicted to the "feel good" consumer culture of our society. Some of us are even addicted to entertaining forms of worship. While coming to church every Sunday, we have become addicts because we are discouraged about making a difference in our world. So instead of trying to do something we sit wasting away in our pity-party of discouragement. Nehemiah and the people participating in the rebuilding of broken communities also knew something about discouragement. In verse 19, we find that Sanballat and Tobiah tried to discourage the rebuilder by laughing at them and ridiculing their work. However when one looks closely at the twentieth verse of the second chapter, we find Nehemiah's answer to discouragement. God always provides the Lord's people with an answer to discouragement. Nehemiah said, "The God of heaven will give us success. We His servants will start rebuilding." (Neh. 2:20).

If we examine this verse closely, we will be able to derive from it, four principles that will teach us how we, as individuals and as a church, can rise up and rebuild the broken places in our lives and communities.

I. Determination

If you are going to rise up and build in the midst of discouragement, you must have determination. If you are going to live a life of joy and power for the Lord, you have got to have determination. You have to be determined to follow the Lord and be obedient to the Lord no matter what anyone else says or thinks. You have got to be determined to love the Lord thy God with all your heart and with all your soul. If we are going to rise up and rebuild in the midst of discouragement, we must be determined.

A biblical example of determination is the story of Esther. When Esther rose to the position of Queen, God used her in a marvelous way to save her people from destruction.

Esther 2:5-8

Now there was in the citadel of Susa a Jew of the tribe of Benjamin, named Mordecai son of Jair, the son of Shimei, the son of Kish, who had been carried into exile from Jerusalem by Nebuchadnezzar king of Babylon, among those taken captive with Jehoiachin king of Judah. Mordecai had a cousin name Hadassah, whom he had brought up because she had neither father nor mother. This girl, who was also known as Esther, was lovely in form and features, and Mordecai had taken her as his own daughter when her father and mother died. When the king's order and edict had been proclaimed, many girls were brought to the citadel of Susa and put under the care of Hegai. Esther also was taken to the king's palace and entrusted to Hegai, who had charge of the harem.

The King of Persia was disappointed in his former wife, Queen Vashti, so he removed her from office and a great contest was held to find a new Queen to please the king. Esther, one of those who had been taken captive when Jerusalem was conquered, was placed in the harem and selected queen. She was no privileged young lady. Esther rose from among an ethnic group of slaves. She was an orphan who was raised by her uncle. God had a plan for Esther in the palace of Susa.

There was a sinister plot to destroy the Jews. A wicked man named Haman had bent the king's ear to his point of view. In doing so, he tricked the king into declaring that all Jews be killed on a given day.

He despised the Jews, and Mordecai, uncle of Esther, because of their faithfulness to God's Will.

Then Esther sent this reply to Mordecai:

Esther 4:15–5:3

"Go, gather together all the Jews who are in Susa, and fast for me. Do not eat or drink for three days, night or day. I and my maids will fast as you do. When this is done, I will go to the king, even though it is against the law. And if I perish, I perish." So Mordecai went away and carried out all of Esther's instructions. On the third day Esther put on her royal robes and stood in the inner court of the palace, in front of the king's hall. The king was sitting on his royal throne in the hall, facing the entrance. When he saw Queen Esther standing in the court, he was pleased with her and held out to her the gold scepter that was in his hand. So Esther approached and touched the tip of the scepter. Then the king asked, "What is it, Queen Esther? What is your request? Even up to half the kingdom, it will be given you." "If it pleases the king," replied Esther, "let the king, together with Haman, come today to a banquet I have prepared for him."

Esther recognized the importance of winning others to her point of view. She knew that it would have been political, and possibly literal, suicide for her to have blurted out her request. Instead, she moved the confrontation to a more comfortable and controllable environment. She decided to woo the king with a meal. After the first meal, she still had little confidence. Therefore, she invited Xerxes and Haman to return for another meal another day. She needed time to make sure that there would be no conflicts with her appeal. She wanted to have the men at ease, and win the king's favor.

Esther 7:1-6

So the king and Haman went to dine with Queen Esther, and as they were drinking wine on that second day, the king again asked, "Queen Esther, what is your petition? It will be given you. What is your request? Even up to half the kingdom, it will be granted." Then Queen Esther answered, "If I have found favor with you, O king, and if it pleases your majesty, grant me my life—this is my petition. And spare my people—this is my request. For I and my people have been sold for destruction and slaughter and annihilation. If we had merely been sold as male and female slaves, I would have kept quiet, because no such distress would justify disturbing the king." King Xerxes asked Queen Esther, "Who is he? Where is the man who has dared to do such a thing?" Esther said, "The adversary and enemy is this vile Haman."

Then Haman was terrified before the king and queen.

Esther prevailed before King Xerxes and saved her people from destruction. She was determined, even though her addressing the king without being previously called to him was an offense punishable by death. She sought God's help in prayer and asked for the prayers of all God's people. With the strength that comes from prayer and fasting, she addressed the problem directly with the king. The evil Haman received his just reward, since he was hung on the very gallows that he had purposed to use on Mordecai.

Like Esther, God's people must be determined if they are to rebuild and be restored. It would have been easy for Queen Hadassah, Queen Esther, to stay there in the lap of luxury, but she determined in her heart that God had positioned her in a special place for a special purpose.

God is Sovereign. He rules in the affairs of people and nations. Therefore, He places his people in strategic places in order to accomplish His Will. Often, we miss opportunities because we were simply not determined to find and follow God's special plan for our lives.

Another example of God placing determined people strategically in position is that of Daniel. He was taken captive when Nebuchadnezzar captured the city of Jerusalem. Yet, he refused to follow the plans of a wicked oppressor. He was determined to follow God.

Daniel 1:3-9

> *Then the king ordered Ashpenaz, chief of his court officials, to bring in some of the Israelites from the royal family and the nobility—young men without any physical defect, handsome, showing aptitude for every kind of learning, well informed, quick to understand, and qualified to serve in the king's palace. He was to teach them the language and literature of the Babylonians. The king assigned them a daily amount of food and wine from the king's table. They were to be trained for three years, and after that they were to enter the king's service. Among these were some from Judah: Daniel, Hananiah, Mishael and Azariah. The chief official gave them new names: to Daniel, the name Belteshazzar; to Hananiah, Shadrach; to Mishael, Meshach; and to Azariah, Abednego. But Daniel resolved not to defile himself with the royal food and wine, and he asked the chief official for permission not to defile himself this way. Now God had caused the official to show favor and sympathy to Daniel.*

II. Discipline

Daniel was determined to follow God's plans for his life. He was also disciplined. All the finest of the young minds of the Hebrew people were taken and put into oppression. The king wanted to train these young men at an early age. He wanted to brainwash them, if you will, so they could be the servants of the oppressor.

We are told that Daniel purposed and determined in his heart that he was not going to break his discipline and eat the king's meat. He was going to stand up for the discipline of God. When he stood up for the discipline of God, he received favor with his enemies. God had a plan for this young man.

We are told that Daniel, and the other children smarter and more handsome than any of the other slaves, stood on the discipline of God and refused to be brainwashed. One of the major problems of the church today is that we are not disciplined. We do not read the Word in a disciplined fashion. We don't pray in a disciplined fashion.

You will never rise up if all you have is a religion of emotionalism, because emotions come and go. Some days you feel like reading the Word and some days you don't. Some days you feel like praying and some days you don't. When you are disciplined by the spirit of God, it does not matter how you feel, you just go ahead and do it anyhow. If we are going to rise up, we must be determined and we must be disciplined.

III. Devoted

We must also be devoted. We have to be devoted to God. Most people who come to church don't really know who they are devoted to. Some people come to church because they are devoted to feeling good. Others come to church because they are devoted to finding a husband or a wife. Still others come because they like to sing in the choir or serve on the usher board. Maybe they like to sit on the front pew of the church or serve as an officer in the church. Perhaps they would rather have a title than a testimony of what God has done for them.

When you are devoted to Almighty God, it doesn't matter what the newspaper says. It doesn't matter what they say on your job. It doesn't matter how much others laugh at you and talk about you, and run you down. When you are devoted to God, you know that God is your Way-maker, your Burden-bearer and the best thing that has ever happened in your life.

When friends leave you, it might hurt you, but you aren't devoted to your friends, you are devoted to God. Your husband may leave you, your wife may leave you, even if everybody else has left, if you hold on to God, God will be devoted to you.

If you want to understand devotion, remember the Bible story about Shadrach, Meshach, and Abednego.

When the king built a statue and ordered that everybody would have to bow down and pray to his statute. The law said that they could not pray to any other god except the statue which the king had made. Shadrach, Meshach, and Abednego were devoted to the one true God.

They could not worship another and they had to worship God. They said, "We will not bow down. You can throw us into the fiery furnace if you want to, but we will not bow down. God may save us from the fiery furnace or we may lose our life in the furnace. Whether God saves us or not, we are going to be devoted to the Lord." That's devotion.

Daniel 3:19-28

Then Nebuchadnezzar was furious with Shadrach, Meshach and Abednego, and his attitude toward them changed. He ordered the furnace heated seven times hotter than usual and commanded some of this strongest soldiers in his army to tie up Shadrach, Meshach and Abednego and throw them into the blazing furnace. So these men, wearing their robes, trousers, turbans and other clothes, were bound and thrown into the blazing furnace. The king's command was so urgent and the furnace so hot that the flames of the fire killed the soldiers who took up Shadrach, Meshach and Abednego, and these three men, firmly tied, fell into the blazing furnace. Then King Nebuchadnezzar leaped to his feet in amazement and asked his advisers, "Weren't there three men that we tied up and threw into the fire?" They replied, "Certainly, O king." He said, "Look! I see four men walking around in the fire, unbound and unharmed, and the fourth looks like a son of the gods." Nebuchadnezzar then approached the opening of the blazing furnace and shouted, "Shadrach, Meshach and Abednego, servants of the Most High God, come out! Come here!" So Shadrach, Meshach and Abednego came out of the fire, and the satraps, prefects, governors and royal advisers crowded around them. They saw that the fire had not harmed their bodies, nor was a hair of their heads singed; their robes were not scorched, and there was no smell of fire on them. Then Nebuchadnezzar said, "Praise be to the God of Shadrach, Meshach and Abednego, who has sent his angel and rescued his servants! They trusted in Him and defied the king's command and were willing to give up their lives rather than serve or worship any god except their own God.

Some of us are only devoted to God as long as he puts food on our table, clothes on our back, and a roof over our heads. Real devotion is being able to praise God when you've got cancer. It is being able to praise God when you have just lost your job. Devotion is the ability to praise God when you have to miss a meal. That's devotion.

If you want to understand devotion, consider Job. He lost all his material wealth and all his children died. When he also lost all of his health, his wife encouraged him to, "Curse God and die." Job had been devoted to God all of his life. He knew that he came into this world naked, alone, and without possessions and was willing to leave this world the same way. He knew that his bounty was at God's disposal rather than his. That's devotion.

Job 1:21-22

> *And* [Job] *said: "Naked I came from my mother's womb, and naked I will depart. The Lord gave and the Lord has taken away; may the name of the Lord be praised." In all this, Job did not sin by charging God with wrongdoing.*

If we are going to rise up, we have got to be determined. If we are going to rise up, we have got to be disciplined. If we are going to rise, we have got to be devoted. When you put all three of these things together, the Lord will deliver you.

IV. Deliverance

Nehemiah knew that God in Heaven would prosper Jerusalem. He didn't look to the king for deliverance.

He didn't say that social services would do it. We cannot look to the Democratic or Republican party, the NAACP, the Urban League, the wealth of the Japanese, or anyone else. God will prosper us. If you are going to be delivered, you better take your eyes off that man, take your eyes off that woman, job, career, profession take your eyes off of City Hall, take your eyes off the Governor and fix your eyes on God. The Lord will deliver the broken cities of our land. The Lord will deliver the broken lives.

Nehemiah didn't care how much other laughed. He wasn't concerned about scorn or ridicule. He was determined to rise up and build. We are going to rise up and build.

Perhaps your life is in trouble. Maybe you have become destitute because of your addiction to substance abuse. Perhaps your life is torn apart with crack and alcohol. Maybe you have been involved in prostitution. Perhaps your marriage is in deep trouble. You could be a student with an IQ of 140, but you can only make F's in school. The Lord wants to deliver you.

The Lord wants to deliver you whatever your problem is. The Lord wants you to say, "I will rise up." It doesn't matter what discouragement says. When discouragement comes knocking at your door, just say "I'm going to rise up and build. I'm going to build my family. I'm going to build my spiritual life. I'm going to build up black men. I'm going to build up the black family. I'm going to build up the church."

How are we going to reach the masses? Jesus is the key. He'll draw the drug addict. He'll draw the prostitute. He'll draw the alcoholic. He'll draw the middle class people who have forgotten from where they came. He'll draw even you. Jesus said:

Matthew 11:28-30

Come to Me, all you who are weary and burdened, and I will give you rest. Take My yoke upon you and learn from Me, for I am gentle and humble in heart and you will find rest for your souls. For My yoke is easy and My burden is light.

Broken lives are the specialty of the Master. He wants us to come to Him. He will build us up. He will strengthen us. He will give us the character to reshape the face of our cities. He was the hope of Nehemiah. He was the hope of Jerusalem in Nehemiah's day. He is the hope of our cities. We will rise up. We will rebuild. We will be restored.

Review and Application

1. What do you think are some of the attitudes of people living in communities broken by drugs, crime, violence and poverty?

2. What attitude will overcome discouragement?

3. What character trait, if developed, will help us overcome the tendency to live by our feelings?

4. Where must we place our devotion if we will succeed at rebuilding?

Chapter 4

The Purpose of the Church

Nehemiah 3:1 KJV

Then Eliashib the high priest rose up with his brethren the priest, and they builded the sheep gate; they sanctified it, and set up the doors of it, even unto the tower of Meah they sanctified it unto the tower of Hananeel.

What is the purpose of the local church? How sad it is that people are born, baptized, married, and buried in a church, and they often don't know what the purpose of the church really is. How sad it is that for years people look forward to coming to Sunday worship with a shallow understanding of God's church. They dress up Sunday after Sunday. They come to pay their tithes and give their offerings. They sing and shout and go back home and still fail to recognize the purpose of the church.

How sad it is that many people claim that they are called to preach the gospel of Jesus Christ and spend 20, 30, 40 and sometimes even 50 years in the ministry, and they still don't know what the purpose of the local church is. Jesus said:

Matthew 5:13-16

You are the salt of the earth. But if the salt loses its saltiness, how can it be made salty again? It is no longer good for anything, except to be thrown out and trampled by men. You are the light of the world. A city on a hill cannot be hidden. Neither do people light a lamp and put it under a bowl. Instead they put it on its stand and it gives light to everyone in the house. In the same way, let your light shine before men, that they may see your good deeds and praise your Father in heaven.

Look at the confusion that exists in our cities. For example, when one looks at the confusion that exists in our nation, and world, it is directly related to the fact that those whom Christ calls the salt of the earth and the light of the world, don't know what their purpose is or the purpose of the church.

You would expect the world to be confused if those who are supposed to be leading the world to God don't know their own purpose. One of the reasons that many of our families in the African American community are falling apart is that drugs are destroying the best of our young minds. Indeed, almost an entire generation is falling into the trap of substance abuse. This is the reason that there are more black men in prison than there are in college. This is the reason that men and women do not get along together. These issues are directly related to the fact that we do not understand our purpose and the purpose of the local church.

When believers do not understand their purpose, the devil and the principalities and powers have a "field day." One thing the devil is very clear on is, he knows his purpose. His purpose is to steal and to destroy. Jesus said, "The thief comes only to steal and kill and destroy; I have come that they may have life, and have it to the full" (Jn. 10:10).

While we in the church are selling chicken dinners, having fashion shows, conducting bingo games, and taking trips to Atlantic City, all the while fussing about which Board is going to be in charge or who is going to be the president of the organization, the enemy is still focused. The Apostle Peter issued a severe warning to the early church that stands true today,

1 Peter 5:8-9

> *Be self-controlled and alert. Your enemy the devil prowls around like a roaring lion looking for someone to devour. Resist him, standing firm in the faith, because you know that your brothers throughout the world are undergoing the same kinds of sufferings.*

While we are fussing about things that do not matter, our children are dying. Our cities are decaying, our relationships are failing. Our families are becoming more and more divided because we do not understand the purpose of the local church.

We find in Nehemiah that God is trying to remind us of the true purpose of the local church, in the Old

Testament model of the priesthood and the Temple. God is using this Old Testament model to remind the church of its true purpose and to remind every believer who is a member of a church of their purpose. For the church is just not a building. The church is every living member that claims to belong to the body of Christ. In reality, where you live, where you work, and where you go, that is where the church is. The church is not brick and mortar, but the church is flesh and blood. The church is the soul and body of people who have come to trust Christ for their salvation and have bonded to a local assembly.

We see in Nehemiah that God is giving us insight into the local church and our purpose within the church. We found that the walls of Jerusalem had been broken down prior to Nehemiah's day. The walls are symbolic of the fact that the family structure and the spirit of the people have been destroyed. After Nehemiah had shared with them the plan to rebuild the walls, the people said, "Let us rise and build." Next, we find that they have moved to the reality of actually building.

It is one thing to talk about rebuilding. We have a lot of churches, a lot of preachers, and a lot of politicians that talk about rebuilding. The issue is not how well you talk and how rhetorical you are, the issue is can you bring that rhetoric into reality. That is why churches must no longer focus just on preaching and teaching, but our preaching and teaching must focus on empowering our members to bring the Word of God into reality.

Nehemiah 3:1 KJV

Then Eliashib, the High Priest, rose up with his brethren, the priests, and they builded the sheep gate. They sanctified it and set up the doors of it.

Every person began to rebuild a section of the wall. The Bible explains that Eliashib the High priest rose up with his brethren, the priests, and they built the sheep gate and sanctified it. In other words, the leaders in the rebuilding process were not the politicians. They were not the educators. The rebuilders were the spiritual leaders of the community. Eliashib and those who worked with him are role models for all spiritual leaders who are interested in participating in God's plan to rebuild our broken world.

I. Boldness

The only way we are going to be able to rebuild our cities and rebuild our nation is if the spiritual leaders take responsibility for setting the proper example for our community. The fact of the matter is that there must be a partnership between preachers and politicians. Politicians and educators by themselves cannot rebuild the community, they need God who has the power to rebuild.

The local church must be bold. The text says that Eliashib, the High Priest, rose up. It takes boldness to rise up when everybody else is sitting down. It takes boldness to stand up and speak the truth and power of God when everybody is concerned about staying comfortable.

Eliashib could have stayed behind his high priestly garment. He could have used the Word of God to hide from reality. But Eliashib understood that when you belong to God, God wants his men and women to be bold. God wants spiritual leaders who are so bold that they take part in the hard and difficult work of rebuilding the broken places.

What we need today is preachers and members who are bold socially. We have to stand up and take our streets back from the dope dealer, and criminals. In standing up to be bold socially, we must not only take our streets back, but also be bold enough to tell middle class black people that, "You are only one step away from the ghetto you left. If you forget where you came from, all your education and money means nothing unless you are bold enough to reach back and lift somebody else up." We have to be bold socially.

James 2:15-17

Suppose a brother or sister is without clothes and daily food. If one of you says to him, "Go I wish you well; keep warm and well fed," but does nothing about his physical needs, what good is it? In the same way, faith by itself, if it is not accompanied by action, is dead.

We must be bold spiritually. All of the problems that exist—the violence, the drugs, the destruction of the black family, and incest—they are symptoms of a spiritual problem. When any people, any city, and any nation turn their backs on God, then that is the beginning of the end of those people and that nation.

As long as black people had little materially, we had time for God, but, as soon as we got a little money in our pockets and had more than one or two suits, and dresses, and were able to move out of our row houses, and got more education, then we forgot about God. Whatever you have, you got it not because of how good you are, or how smart you are, but because the grace of God opened doors for you that would not have otherwise been opened. We have to be bold spiritually.

To be bold spiritually is to be able to tell others that the wages of sin is death. Sin is not just your sexual preference. When you do not take time to help the poor, that is sin. When you do not take time to educate children who have only a single parent, that is sin. When you come to church every Sunday, and pass the hungry and homeless people around the doors, that is sin. When you sit next to somebody,

Sunday after Sunday, but think you are too cute and too important to speak, that is sin.

The purpose of the local church is to train people how to be bold. The church is to be bold when it comes to facing social and spiritual issues as well as proclaiming the truth of the gospel. The leaders of the church must be bold as they are given as gifts to the church, not so that the congregation can sit and wait for them to do all the work, but so that the congregation can be equipped to boldly rise socially and spiritually. A bold church prepares us to rebuild.

II. Build

The purpose of the local church is to be bold. The purpose of the local church is also to build-up. A lot of churches specialize in tearing folk down. Any time you go to a church where there are members that specialize in tearing people down, that is not a Church of God. That is the church of the devil.

You don't have to come to church to tear people down. They do it on television. They do it in the newspaper. We do it to each other. If we are going to be the church of Jesus Christ, we have to build others up. We build people up by being encouraging and positive instead of discouraging and negative. We build people up by telling them they can do better. You can achieve excellence in and through Christ Jesus.

We must take this black man who has been down so long and so low and tell him that God loves him no matter what he has done. Regardless of what the newspapers say, we have to build that brother up.

We have to take this black woman that has worked from sun up to sun down who is continually maligned and misused and abused, and tell her "Sister you look good. You are good. You are the best thing that ever happened. We are going to protect you and we are going to provide for you. We are going to make a way for you because you are our queen and God gave you to us." We must build this woman up. We have to build our young people up. They think they have to look like someone else to be important. They try to act like somebody else and talk like somebody else. We need to tell them that, "you are black and you are beautiful whether you are light and half white or black as midnight, you have the blood of Jesus running through your veins." We must build them up.

We have to build our single parents up. We have to build the black family up. There is no such thing as an illegitimate child. God doesn't make illegitimate children. If you are a single parent, you don't have to raise your child by yourself because, if you put your hand in God's hands, you will be able to sing, "I'm never alone. He's my Brother, He's my Father. He will make a way for you and me." We must build up.

The book of Nehemiah explains that not only do they rise up, but they also build up. If you put broken people in new buildings, they will tear them up. Look at the projects. The projects were beautiful when they were first built, but when you put poor people who are broken and have never been taught that they are somebody in the sight of God, those broken people will tear down the good that you give them. However, if you build them up on the inside, they may not have a penthouse, but if they know that they are a child of God, their homes and streets will be the cleanest you can see.

Ephesians 4:11-13 KJV

It was He who gave some to be apostles, some to be prophets, some to be evangelists, and some to be pastors and teachers, to prepare God's people for works of service, so that the body of Christ may be built up until we all reach unity in the faith and in the knowledge of the Son of God and became mature, attaining to the whole measure of the fullness of Christ.

The purpose of the local church is to train people and demonstrate how to be builders, building each other up. We are to build one another up. We find strength in the fellowship of other believers. We find advice and counsel from others who have faced our problems before. We feast on the Word of God and are filled with the Spirit of God. There can be no substitute for God's people building one another up in Him.

III. Believe

Finally, Eliashib was able to be a role model of boldness and building because he believed in God. Today, our job is to believe. Not in what the newspaper says, because if you believe in what the newspapers say, the condition of our people and the condition of our city and the condition of our nation appear to be hopeless, but, when you believe in God, you know that God can take nothing and make something out of it.

The Scriptures remind us that we are no longer simply strangers on the earth. God's people are called to be special in His sight. We are set apart from the world because we are His chosen ones. No longer can we claim simply a worldly heritage and inheritance, but we have a kingdom heritage and inheritance in Christ.

1 Peter 2:9-10

> *But you are a chosen people, a royal priesthood, a holy nation, a people belonging to God, that you may declare the praises of Him who called you out of darkness and into His wonderful light. Once you were not a people, but now you are the people of God: once you had not received mercy, but now you have received mercy.*

If you look closely at the text in Nehemiah, it says that Eliashib, the High Priest, rose up with his

Brethren, the priests, and they built the sheep gate and then they sanctified it. Why did they sanctify it. Even though everything had been broken down around them, they believed that God still had all power in his hands. When you believe in God, you sanctify the little bit that you have and you turn it over to the Lord.

God is looking for men and women that specialize in doing the impossible. He is looking for people who will be bold, both socially and spiritually, for those who will build one another up rather than tear each other down, and for those who will dare to believe that what He says is true regardless of the circumstances. God is looking for people who are bold enough to believe that the broken places and broken people can be rebuilt.

Review and Application

1. How can we become role models in God's plan of rebuilding broken lives like Eliashib?

2. What kinds of boldness do you think the church must exhibit?

3. What kinds of things can you do to help build others up?

4. How do you think the impossible can be accomplished?

Chapter 5

The Battle
for the Mind

Nehemiah 4:6 KJV

So built we the wall. And all the wall was joined together unto the half thereof: for the people had a mind to work.

It does not take in intense or in depth study of African history to know that African people are a people who have a mind to work. For anyone who has done even a surface reading of African history and ancient African civilizations know that we come from a people who are builders. We come from a people who have a long heritage of working and working hard. We are the builders of pyramids. We are the builders of the first civilizations. Indeed, the first great civilizations.

George G.M. James in his major text "Stolen Legacy" teaches us that geometry, medicine, philosophy, and more, began in Africa. We are a people who have a mind to work. The ancient kingdom of Timbuktu in the thirteenth and fourteenth centuries in Africa had the greatest university known to man. But when Arabs conquered Timbuktu, they burned and destroyed the libraries because they did not want people to know that we were a people who had a mind to work. They did not want us to know that we were a people who were builders and had a long tradition of building.

Even when slavery came into the African continent; even when the Europeans broke into the West Coast of Africa, even when over 10 million persons were snatched from the African continent, many of their bones lie on the floor of the Atlantic Ocean, even after having endured 300-400 hundred years of the most intense slavery that the world had ever seen, our people still had a mind to work.

During slavery we were the finest of artisans. We were the finest of builders. We built the churches. We did the steel work. We were the great cooks and the restaurant people. We were the people who had the skills. After we were supposedly freed by the Emancipation Proclamation, a man by the name of Booker T. Washington had a mind to work and built Tuskegee, one of the finest educational institutions that the world had ever seen. From that grew businesses and insurance companies and magazines and newspapers. Many of which are now closed or on the verge of closing. While our people just out of slavery had a mind to work, something has happened to us in our recent history where we have lost our mind to work.

When we look at the fourth chapter of Nehemiah we ask, why could the people rebuild the broken places in their lives? Because they had a mind to work. If one looks at the Hebrew closely, a better translation would not be that they had a mind to work, the better translation would be that they worked with all of their hearts.

Something happened to them on the inside that made them willing to change their condition on the outside. That is the reason that we, individually and as a people and a nation, are in the condition that we are in. It is because there is something wrong with us on the inside. Something is wrong that degrees and designer clothes and German and Japanese cars cannot hide. Something that living in split-level homes in the Country and in the regentrified neighborhoods of our city cannot hide. There is something deeply wrong inside of us. There is something wrong with our heart. There is something wrong with our minds.

If one looks at our condition today, one would say that we as a people have a mind to kill. When one looks at all of the young men and women that are dying on the streets of our nation, and understands that the numbers are continuing to increase, one could easily make a point that we have a mind to kill.

When one looks at our neighborhoods, just because one lives in a poor neighborhood does not mean that one has to be dirty and uncaring. One could say that we have a mind to destroy what we do have. Some who live in middle class comfort may think, "Well Reverend you are talking about them other folks." However, there is something wrong in our hearts. If one looks at how we mishandle what God has given us, one would say that we have a mind of self-hatred. That we have a mind of criticism. That we have a mind to pull each other down.

Therefore, the question that faces us as a church today is "How do we move from having a negative, destructive, uncommitted mind, to having a mind that is fixed on doing the will of God?

As I considered this question, I began with a book I believe is a very important book by Jonathan Kozol, "Savage Inequalities." In that text I saw why and what this culture and this world is doing to destroy our children and to put a negative spirit in our children so that they will never have the mind to build. The book, "Savage Inequalities" is about how the public education system is a system rooted in race and class.

If you are black and poor, you receive the worst materials, the worst teachers, and the worst education nationwide. If you happen to be white and rich, or black and middle class, and know how to work the system, then you are able to get into magnet schools. Instead we put a mind set into poor children and into their families where they don't know how to use the public education system that is supposed to be for all children and all families. Brother Kozol says, "Children, of course, don't understand at first that they are being cheated. They come to school with a degree of faith and optimism. And they often seem to thrive during the first few years. It is sometimes not until the third grade, that the teachers start to see the warning signs of failure. By the fourth grade, many children see it too. These kids are aware of their failures. Says a fourth grade teacher in Chicago, 'Some of them act like the game's already over.' By the fifth or sixth grade, many children demonstrate their loss of faith by staying out of school."

The system is rigged to rob our children and to rob us of our faith in the ability that God has given us to make a difference and change the world. This is not only true of those children in poor neighborhoods. If you look at yourself and your family compared to your dreams and what you once wanted to achieve in your life, and for your community, you would truthfully say, you have lost your faith.

You have lost your optimism because the entire culture is seeking to rob us of a mind that will work. They want us to kill ourselves. They want us to be in prison. They want us to say that we can never be anything, never do anything. They want those of us who have talent and ability to say, "I've got mine, and you've got yours." They want us to have a mind that is lazy and will not work.

God is saying to us, we had better check out our minds. What kind of mind do you have today? Don't compare yourself to anybody else. Are you tutoring some children who cannot read or write? Check out your mind. You have raised your children. Are you willing to think about adopting a black boy or black girl who could use your experience and use the money that you thought you had set aside for another vacation? You set it aside for a vacation, but God set it aside so you could help some child to live a victorious life.

Check out your mind. Are you the one who always talks about what African Americans should do for each other, but you go to somebody else's law firm, somebody else's tax man, somebody else's builder, somebody else's college, and somebody else's church. Check out your mind.

Where do you shop? Where do you bank? Where do you save? How do you talk to your husband? Your wife? How do you talk to the person that sits next to you in church every Sunday? Check out your mind.

That's why the old folks say He's a heart fixer and a mind regulator. They understood that when you just get so high that you think that you can make it by yourself, when you get a little education and a little money, that your mind gets all mixed up. Education doesn't give you integrity. Money does not give you integrity. You have got to have something on the inside that controls your heart and controls your mind.

What is wrong with us today is that we are crazy, mixed up, and messed up in the mind? Now that we know the problem, how do we change our mind? How do we rediscover the mind to work?

I. Confidence

A mind to work is a mind that is filled with confidence. We have lost our confidence. We aren't sure about ourselves anymore. If you want to recapture your confidence, you better recapture a relationship with the Lord. Sisters, if you don't have confidence, don't expect a man to give it to you. Only God can give you confidence. You will never have a good relationship until you have confidence in yourselves, until you love yourselves.

Brothers you will never be the king of your house and the king of your neighborhood until you walk like a king, talk like a king, and think like a king. A king doesn't just wear nice clothes and have a pocket full of money. A king knows I'm a child of the most high God and I'm going to walk right and talk right because I have confidence in myself.

We need to raise our children with confidence. Our children can do anything anyone else's children can do. They can be successful at math, science and geometry. If Michael Jordan can turn in the air in geometric circles, and figure out how to dunk that basketball, your son and our daughter can figure out how to get better grades.

You must give them confidence. Tell them they are the smartest children in the world. Tell them they are of the best in the world. Then expect them to act like it. Give them confidence. That mind will not only become a confident mind, it will be a constructive mind.

II. Constructive

A mind to work is a constructive mind. A constructive mind looks at obstacles and sees opportunities. A constructive mind looks at the problems caused by broken lives and broken communities and sees possibilities to build something new and better. A constructive mind hears: No we can't but responds, Yes, we can. We specialize in tearing each other down. We specialize in looking for the worst. When you have a mind to work, you can look at the worst situation possible and see something constructive in it.

If you have God on your side, you can say with God, "I can do all things through Christ that strengthens me." Stop running yourself down. Stop running your people down. Stop running your church down. Recognize that God will make a positive and powerful difference.

III. Committed

A mind to work is a mind that is confident, constructive, and committed. Rebuilding is not a 100-yard dash. It's a marathon affair. We as a people must recover our sense of commitment. Do you want to know why civil rights organizations are going down? They have problems, but so do you. Do you know why with all the people who have graduated from Morgan, Fisk, and Howard Universities, that these schools have some of the lowest endowments in all of America? Do you have the answer? It is because we are a people that lack commitment, we aren't committed to anything but selfishness. We are committed to the next dress, pair of shoes, or car. We are committed to material things. Until we are committed to God we can't commit to doing the right thing.

If you want to have a mind that will work and build, you have got to learn how to be committed to God. That is why men can't be committed to women, women can't be committed to men, children can't be committed to their parents, parents can't be committed to their children, church folks can't be committed to the Church of God, because we have lost our sense of commitment. We must regain the spiritual tenacity revealed in commitment to God.

Our mind must be confident. This mind must be constructive, this mind must be committed and finally this mind must be conscious.

IV. Consciousness

When Dr. James Washington from Union Theological Seminary was at Bethel, we were up late talking one night about the condition of our community and why all of this killing was taking place. Jim said it is because we have lost our God-consciousness.

There is a difference between Church-consciousness and God-consciousness. There was a time when even those outside of the church knew that there were some things that they would just not do because they said, "God wouldn't like that." Now we have lost our God-consciousness. People curse in the church. People smoke in the sanctuary. People say anything and do anything anywhere they want in God's House. We have lost our God-consciousness. If you want a mind that works and revere, "Let this mind be in you that was in Christ Jesus." He had a committed mind.

Romans 12:2 KJV

And be not conformed to this world: but be ye transformed by the renewing of your mind, that ye may prove what is that good, and acceptable, and perfect, will of God.

Now that you know the answer to the problem it is not enough to just know the answer, you must live the answer. The answer by itself is not going to change your condition. That is why some of you want a fairy tale religion. You want a magical promise that things will change before you leave the church. If you trust God, you will be able to say, "Be not dismayed what ere betide, God will take care of you."

I don't care how many people the Governor lays off. I don't care whether the administration extends certain benefits. If you have checked out your mind, you will be able to sing, "Beneath His wings, His love abides. God will take care of you." How do you think you are where you are today, when you couldn't take care of yourself. God took care of you.

The cities are broken, but God will use us to rebuild and restore. Restoration comes as each one of us begins to have a mind to work. We must put all of our hearts into doing what God has called us to do. We can and we shall.

Review and Application

1. Describe the rich African-American heritage and how it has changed.

2. List some steps you would take to build confidence in a child?

3. What must our minds be committed to?

4. What is the difference between Christ-consciousness and Church-consciousness?

Chapter 6

A Combative Spirituality

Nehemiah 4:7-9 KJV

But it came to pass, that when Sanballat and Tobiah and the Arabians, and the Ammonites, and the Ashododites, heard that the walls of Jerusalem were made up, and that the breaches began to be stopped, that they were very wroth, and conspired all of them together to come and to fight against Jerusalem, and to hinder it. Nevertheless we made our prayer unto our God, and set a watch against them day and night, because of them.

ornel West is the head of the African American Studies Department at Princeton University. He also happens to be one of the sharpest and keenest minds anywhere in our nation. Cornel is a Christian who also is an intellectual whom God has called to exercise his ministry on the college campus. His first book of essays was entitled "Prophetic Fragments."

The first essay is a speech that he presented at the Library of Congress on the life of Dr. Martin Luther King, Jr. In this specific paper he has a phrase that gripped my attention when I first received a copy of the books some years ago—combative spirituality.

In it he focuses on the importance of Dr. King's combative spirituality. He explained how it was this combative spirituality that allowed African Americans to survive in America. As I began to think about that phrase, I wondered whether or not it had any place in Scripture.

I wondered whether by looking at God's Word we could find any example of a combative spirituality.

Then I began to raise questions such as, Why is a combative spirituality necessary? What does a combative spirituality look like? What are the components of a combative spirituality. When I began the study of the Book of Nehemiah it became clear that God was beginning to answer the questions that I had about this combative spirituality.

Nehemiah 4:7-9 KJV

But it came to pass that when Sanballat and Tobiah and the Arabians and the Ammonites and the Ashdodites heard that the walls of Jerusalem were made up and that the breaches began to be stopped, then they were wroth. And conspired, all of them together, to come and to fight against Jerusalem and to hinder it. Nevertheless, we made our prayer unto our God and set a watch against them day and night because of them.

Here in the fourth chapter of the Book of Nehemiah, we find that the people had begun to rebuild the broken places. They had begun to rebuild their broken society and their broken lives. We find that these people who had been discouraged and depressed had moved from their depression and were now working together for the deliverance of their people. Anytime you begin to work your way out of your depression, anytime you refuse to be imprisoned behind the invisible bars of discouragement, your enemies get angry.

The more the people began to build, the angrier their enemies got. They began to talk derisively and negatively about what the people of God were doing. They began to put them down and to play the spiritual "dozens." There is in the sixth verse we find that the people of God had a change of mind. It did not matter how negative and discouraging the remarks of their enemies were, they had a mind to work.

The more you try to stay on a positive agenda, the angrier people get who are on a negative agenda. Beginning there in the seventh verse, we are told that the enemies of God, the enemies of the people of God, those who were saying and doing these discouraging things, were very angry. Can you remember how some people that once were your friends, as long as you were doing wrong, seem to lose their friendship once you turn to do right?

It was acceptable for you to stand on the streets and get involved in all kinds of illicit activities as far as those old friends were concerned. They enjoyed watching you suffer through the bondages of this world. However, as soon as you gave your life to God and determined that you were going to try and do the right thing, they became combative. Those people that were always there to encourage you to do wrong are now your worst enemies instead of your best friends. Instead of being happy for you, instead of being happy that you have changed your life, instead of being happy that you are trying to walk in a positive direction, they are angry.

They say things like, "Don't you remember when you used to?" They begin to throw up negative things that you used to do in your face. "Don't you get so high up, remember I knew you when. You know that I know who you slept with, where you slept with him. I know it all." Instead of being positive and trying to reinforce the good that you are doing, the better you do, the angrier they become.

When Nehemiah led the people to do right and rebuild the city, the enemies of the people of God got mad because God was blessing them. Folks get angry the more you get blessed. The better you do on the job, the more traps they set for you. The better you are doing in your family relationship, the more gossip they spread about you and your family. The closer you get to God, the more some church folk talk about you. They put your name in the street because they are just angry.

They do not have enough sense to know that the devil is using them to try to pull you back into the hell you once lived. The enemies of Jerusalem were angry to the point that, in the ninth verse, they conspired to come and fight against Jerusalem and to hinder the rebuilding work.

The more you try and live for God, the harder the forces of evil will come together to fight against you and what you are trying to do for God. They will put everything in your path to hinder you from getting to church—hinder you from worshipping God, hinder you from going to the prayer meeting, hinder you from growing in the knowledge of God. Even the devil will try to hinder you in church from doing God's Word.

All that is evil and demonic will conspire to use every trick in the book to hinder you from growing in the Lord. The devil does not care if you just attend church. However, the devil does not want you to get a hold of faith. The devil does not want you to get a hold of joy. The devil does not want you to get a hold of power. So the devil will put you next to somebody that hinders you from getting a hold of what God brought you to church for in the first place. Somebody will write you a note just at the moment the Word is saying something you need to hear. You will focus your eye on somebody's hips, or somebody's good looks just at the moment that you need to set your eyes on God. The world specializes in trying to hinder us from hearing God. That is why we need to have a combative spirituality.

We are involved in a spiritual warfare. If you are a believer, if you are a disciple of the Lord, we are involved in a spiritual warfare. Satan will use all of his power to make you a victim and put you in the spiritual hospital so you will never be able to grow in the spirit and the power of Almighty God.

Ephesians 6:12-17

For our struggle is not against flesh and blood, but against the rulers, against the authorities, against the powers of this dark world and against the spiritual forces of evil in the heavenly realms. Therefore put on the full armor of God, so that when the day of evil comes, you may be able to stand your ground, and after you have done everything, to stand. Stand firm then, with the belt of truth buckled around your waist, with the breastplate of righteousness in place, and with your feet fitted with the readiness that comes from the gospel of peace. In addition to all this, take up the shield of faith, with which you can extinguish all the flaming arrows of the evil one. Take the helmet of salvation and the sword of the Spirit, which is the word of God.

God has not only called us to combative spirituality, but He has also prepared us for it. There can be no doubt that believers are to stand for the truths of God's Word and look to Him in the face of opposition.

The lessons we learn from Nehemiah's experience *will change us forever.* In the ninth verse we get a description of the components of a combative spirituality. Every time a distraction comes into your life what you must learn how to say is "nevertheless."

When your spiritual enemies would say to you, "I remember when you used to do," All you need to say to yourself is "nevertheless." When they tell you where you used to go and how you used to act, all you need to say is, "That's right, but 'nevertheless.'" When the devil tries to put you back into the prison of negativity say, "I know I used to be this, I used to be that, but 'nevertheless' I am with God, God has changed my life." There in the ninth verse it said, "nevertheless we made our pray[er]."

I. Pray

Number I, if we are going to have a combative spirituality, you have got to know how to pray. We do a lot of talking about praying in the church. We need to talk less about prayer and talk more to God. Because if you look closely in the 9th Verse, it says we make our prayer unto our God. Who do you pray to? I have been in church long enough to know that some folk pray to themselves. Some folk pray to be heard by other people, all of these pretty words. In fact some preachers don't pray, they preach prayers because they want to make folk feel good. But prayer is not suppose to be directed at people. That is why some of us don't have power in our prayers. But when you are involved in a combative spirituality, you have got to learn to call God up for yourself. It is alright to have prayer partners, but you need to learn how to say for yourself, it's me, it's me, oh God standing in the need of prayer. It's alright to ask your pastor to pray for you, but every now and then you have got to know how to fall on your knees and say God, this is Jim, this is Joan. I'm Your child, God and I'm calling on Your name because I need Your joy. I need Your power. I need Your help. Lord, come see about me.

If we ever needed prayer before, we need to pray now. There is danger on every hand. Our children are in danger. Our men are in danger. Our women are in danger. And the only way to protect them in the midst of that danger is to learn how to pray. Before your child goes to school in the morning, pray for them. Before your husband or wife leaves for work, pray for them. Because there is power in prayer.

II. Practical

This combative spirituality, component number I is prayer. Number II, this combative spirituality is practical. Have you ever known folk who are so spiritual that they are no earthly good? But here in the 9th Verse, we learn that a combative spirituality is a practical spirituality because it says nevertheless we made our prayer unto our God and set a watch. In other words, they prayed to God but after they prayed they took practical steps to take care of themselves. The reason that God gives you a mind to think is that after you talk to God, God wants you to use your mind so that you will be able to plan a strategy that will protect your family and protect your children. What is wrong with the church today is that we spend so much time praying that we forgot that we have to pray and be practical.

Someone is saying Rev. give me an example. If you are a student and you have been in school all semester long and you come to your pastor and say Rev. I'm going to fast and pray for the next three days that I pass my final exams. But if you have not studied all semester long, don't blame God when you still get an "F", there is nothing wrong with God, it's that you prayed but you weren't practical. And that is what's wrong with us in the church. Some of us are so spiritual but we are not practical. And when you have a combative spirituality, you pray but you're practical.

III. God Will Protect

What is the next component of this combative spirituality? The third one is not only did they set a watch, but they understood that God will protect you. In fact, I found that God is the best protector because, parents, no matter how much you try and protect your children, you can't be with them all the time. You can't be there with them every time somebody tries to offer them drugs. You can't be there every time somebody tries to get them involved in sex before marriage. But I found out that if you introduce your children to God, God will protect them whether you are with them or not. And that is why you and I today need to learn how to follow God for ourselves.

When you walk with God, God will walk with you. He will protect you in the midst of gangbangers. He will protect you in the midst of rapists. He'll protect you in the midst of being laid off of your job. He'll protect you in the midst of backbiting spirits. He'll protect you in the midst of all hurt, harm and danger. He will be a lamp unto your feet, and a light unto your pathway. How do you know if He will protect you? Well, you would not be here today if the Lord hadn't protected you. He protected you nine months in your mother's womb. He protected you from all hurt, harm and danger. You got clothes on your back, food in your icebox because the Lord has protected you.

IV. The Lord Will Provide

Then finally, the other component of this combative spirituality is that the Lord will provide for you. God will provide. He may not provide what you want, when you want it. But, if you wait on the Lord, they that wait upon the Lord shall renew their strength. They will mount up with wings like eagles. The Lord will provide.

Well, some of you don't believe it. Let me tell you how I know. In the New Testament, it says, "...But my God shall supply all of your needs according to His riches and glory". Don't worry about the economy, you have a Father that has the whole world in His hands. Be not dismayed whatever betides, God will take care of you. Beneath His wings of love he will provide, God will take care of you. When dangers come, God will take care of you.

We can rebuild and restore our lives. We can restore our communities, our cities, and our nations. However, a part of the process will mean being on guard against opposition. There will be those who do not want to see change. They fear change. They are probably uncomfortable with the way things are.

Enemies have a great deal of ammunition to throw at us. We were once like them. We were filled with sin and worldliness. Those who are in Christ are different however. We have been forgiven. In spite of what we once were, God has made us into new creatures. Our goal as individuals and as a church is to conform to the image of Christ. The closer we get to Jesus, the better equipped we will be to combat the ills of our cities.

The nearer we are to Christ, the more our inner wounds and struggles are healed by His touch. As we are restored, we will then be able to restore the broken walls of the city around us. It doesn't matter what the skeptics say. God will prevail and those who are with God will stand for righteousness and justice.

Review and Application

1. What leader in history displayed combative spirituality?

2. What reaction can we expect from others when we begin to change, why?

3. How should we respond to our critics?

4. Where will we receive power to overcome from?

Chapter 7

From Wimps to Warriors

Nehemiah 4:10

And Judah said, The strength of the bearers of burdens is decayed, and there is much rubbish; so that we are not able to build the wall.

One of the benefits of a loving God is that God provides you with the power to rebuild the broken places that exist in our lives and in our communities. Nehemiah knew God's hand in restoration first-hand.

Nehemiah had been blessed with a miraculous audience with King Artaxerxes that ended with him having the king's authority to rebuild Jerusalem. God answered his prayer once again and allowed the people to be of the mind to work and rebuild. He softened the hearts of the Jews to fulfill His plan of restoration. However, every thing worth doing will also have its struggles.

Nehemiah 4:10-14

Meanwhile, the people in Judah said, "The strength of the laborers is giving out, and there is so much rubble that we cannot rebuild the wall." Also our enemies said, "Before they know it or see us, we will be right there among them and will kill them and put an end to the work." Then the Jews who lived near them came and told us ten times over, "Wherever you turn, they will attack us." Therefore I stationed some of the people behind the lowest points of the wall at the exposed places, posting them by families, with their swords, spears and bows. After I looked things over, I stood up and said to the nobles, the officials and the rest of the people, "Don't be afraid of them. Remember the Lord, who is great and awesome, and fight for your brothers, your sons and your daughters, your wives and your homes."

One of the most difficult issues facing the Christian church in America is the perception that Christianity will make you a wimp. When one studies the predominant pictures of Jesus, Christ often appears weak and effeminate. When one hears talk about Jesus, most references are to His weakness and humility. Often people forget about Christ's confrontations with hypocrites and the time he whipped the money changers and ran them from the Temple. The dominant stereotype in the minds of most people seems to be that Christianity is a religion for weaklings.

One of the major reasons that there are not more men, particularly Afro-American men, in the church today, is that men see the church as full of weak people. We have done little to combat the false wimpish stereotype of Christ and Christianity. The church is viewed as a place for weaklings. If we were to take an honest look at most believers in America today, it would be difficult to find those who look more like warriors than wimps.

We tend to always be talking about our problems. We often point to the burdens that we have to bear. The latest defeat is frequently on our minds and lips. Often we conduct negative conversations because, within the church, we have bought into the negative stereotype of believers as wimps.

Anyone who has taken time to read God's Word will understand that God specializes in taking weak people and making them strong. God specializes in taking wimps and turning them into warriors. God takes the defeated and makes them into victors.

The fact is that there is nothing wrong with God, or His dealings with mankind, the problem lies with us. If you have been walking with God for any length of time and you remain a wimp, the problem is not with God. God hasn't changed. God's Word and power are just as real as ever. The problem is with you.

Looking at the fourth chapter of the book of Nehemiah, we find that there were those who looked at the Jews rebuilding Jerusalem as wimps. The world will continually put pressure on believers to make us wimps. Even when God comes into our lives and helps us do something positive, there are those who will want to tear us down and keep us weak.

When we begin to rebuild the broken places in our lives, not everyone will be happy. There is always something or someone out there to challenge us and try to drag us down. One fact about evil is that it never knows how to quit.

Evil is always there trying to steal your strength. Evil wants to steal your power and your joy. Once the people of Nehemiah's time had taken positive steps because they were of the mind to work, the enemy came. They were making great progress. They were encouraged and spirits were high. Then they found a problem.

Problems do not always come from the outside. Often our problems are from within. There is an enemy within and an enemy without. The people of Judah began to lose their self-esteem. They were troubled because the work seemed impossible. There was so much rubble in the way that had to be cleared out. The rubbish was keeping them from making progress on the wall.

Every time we begin to do something positive with our lives, we may begin to hear voices on the inside that tear us down. The nagging thoughts and feelings of depression do not come from God. They are of the enemy, yet they are within us. Every time one gets a vision to do something for God, there will be someone saying, "You can't do that." It is the voice of poor self-esteem. It is the voice of discouragement. It is the voice of frustration. There is a great deal of rubbish on the inside of us that must be cleaned up by the cleansing of the Word of God.

There is something about black people today that keeps us back. It seems that whenever one receives a vision and begins to do something wonderful for God, someone will say, "You are not able to do it." Perhaps it is a husband or wife. Maybe the doubter will be a close friend or brother. The fact remains that as long as you are convinced that you can't do a work for God, you will not be able to do it.

The enemy can start working on the inside. After the enemy within says that you are not able, then the enemy without does his best to stop you. In other words, the enemy will attack from without while we are still dealing with the doubt and frustration that is within. Isn't that what is happening today? We have self-doubt on the inside and dope is attacking our community on the outside. Negative self-images haunt us, and violence attacks us. It is no wonder that people are becoming less and less secure. Where is our security?

Often in the black community, we have become wimps with masters degrees, wimps with nice jobs, wimps with nice homes, and wimps driving nice cars. Nevertheless, we remain wimps because of our insecurity.

We are wimps. We can't even lead our children anymore. Our children tell us what they are going to do instead of us telling them what is permissible. We are wimps. We can't drive the streets of our cities anymore. Children as young as seven and eight years old have become little terrorists making grown men afraid to walk the streets of their own neighborhood. People in church talk about God being our sword and shield, yet we are afraid to go out in the street after the service.

We are wimps. We are afraid of the future. People are afraid of hard economic times. Some say they can't tithe because times are rough. God owns the cattle in a thousand hills. He owns everything. He holds the whole world in His hands. If everyone loses their job, God will still take care of you. Yet, we remain wimps, afraid to move from safety to the risk of faith. How do we move from being wimps to being warriors?

God does not want you to be a wimp. Sister, God does not want you to simply rely on a man for your strength. He wants you to be strong. He wants you to have strength on the inside. Stop being a wimp. Brother, your manhood is not judged by how many babies you make or how many girl friends you have. Your manhood is rooted in the fact that you know God for yourself and you are a child of the King. He is your strength. He wants you to have strength on the inside.

Our children should stop being wimps in the classroom. They can make better than C's and D's.

Their grandparents built the pyramids and the University of Timbuktu. God wants to be your strength. He wants you to have strength on the inside.

How can we stop being wimps? How can we recapture our strength? Nehemiah shows us how to move from wimps to warriors. When Nehemiah heard about the threat from the enemy, he proceeded with a strategy. He sat the people on the walls with spears and swords. They were not going to take any threats sitting down. They were up at the wall and ready to fight.

I. Strategy

You have to have a strategy. What is wrong with us today, as a people, is that we always end up with the wrong strategy. For years we had the Republican strategy. Then we had the Democratic strategy. Some followed the Black Panther strategy. Others stuck with the strategy of the NAACP. Regardless of all of these, you don't need the strategy of men, you need to connect with the strategy of Almighty God.

God's strategy is a family strategy. It may not even be a blood family. It may be the family of the blood of Jesus Christ. Nehemiah placed some people in the lower places and some in the higher places. When I read that, I understood that, before God, no one place is better than another place.

It doesn't matter whether you sit in the front of the church or in back of the church. It matters what spirit you have on the inside. If you came to church because you love the Lord, He can reach you in the balcony or the main floor. It makes no difference to Him. He isn't concerned with our credentials. The Lord doesn't care if you have earned a Ph.D. or no "D." at all. He is concerned with where your heart is.

II. Security

In addition to having a strategy, you must be secure. Wimps are insecure. Nehemiah recognized that the people needed assurance of security. "After I looked things over, I stood up and said to the nobles, the officials and the rest of the people, Don't be afraid of them. Remember the Lord, who is great and awesome, and fight for your brothers, your sons and your daughters, your wives and your homes" (Neh. 4:14).

He told the people not to be afraid of the enemies who were boasting of their exploits. Wimps are afraid of their own shadows. That is what is wrong with us in the church. We are afraid of everything. It is time to be secure. Security does not come by buying an electronic alarm system for your car or your house. Security comes from having the Lord on the inside.

When the Lord secures you, they can steal your car and your house but they can't steal Christ from your heart. They can steal your clothes, but can't steal your salvation that the Lord has clothed you with. When you are secure in the Lord people can talk about you, your husband can lose his job, you can lose your job, your spouse can leave you, but when you are not afraid the Lord will secure you.

God's word, prayer and spiritual discipline are three keys to spiritual security. The broken world in which we live will continue to try to shake us up and make us feel insecure. Fear will make us insecure. Fear of change, fear of ridicule, fear of what people might say and do can make us feel insecure. Fear of being different will often make us compromise and conform to the wrong values and activities. It is God's Word that reminds us that our security is not in people but in God.

Psalm 118:5-9

In my anguish I cried to the Lord, and he answered by setting me free. The Lord is with me: I will not be afraid. What can man to do me? The Lord is with me; he is my helper, I will look in triumph over my enemies. It is better to take refuge in the Lord than to trust in man. It is better to take refuge in the Lord than trust in princes.

III. Spiritually Connected

We need God's strategy and security. We also need to make sure we are spiritually connected. Nehemiah reminded the people to remember the Lord, and not to fear an enemy. As we begin to remember all the things God has done for us in the past, we gain confidence that He will overcome for us in the present. That is why the devil does not want you to read God's Word. The enemy does not want you to think about the blessings of God and the times he delivered you from problems and crisis.

2 Timothy 3:12-17

In fact, everyone who wants to live a godly life in Christ Jesus will be persecuted, while evil men and imposters will go from bad to worse, deceiving and being deceived. But as for you, continue in what you have learned and have become convinced of, because you know those from whom you learn it, and how from infancy you have known the holy Scriptures, which are able to make you wise for salvation through faith in Christ Jesus. All Scripture is God-breathed and is useful for teaching, rebuking, correcting and training in righteousness, so that the man of God may be thoroughly equipped for every good work.

When you remember the goodness of Jesus and what He has done for you, you receive power and strength to carry on. You are able to move forward because you can look back and see that He has helped you so many times before. Maybe He gave you a job when you needed it. Perhaps He brought healing to your body and soul. Maybe God allowed you to be in just the right place to receive a blessing. Through all the struggles and rough times, God has made a way some how.

When you need to be reconnected to Christ, simply remember all the great things He has done for you. Look at His Word and see what He has done for others who were in similar situations. God is the source of our strategy, strength, and security. We must remain spiritually connected if we are to succeed.

You are alive today because the Lord made a way for you. You have clothes on your back today because the Lord made a way for you. You have a roof over your head today because the Lord made a way for you. Don't forget the Lord. You must remember Him.

IV. Stand-Up

If we are going to move from wimps to warriors, we must have a strategy, we must be secure, we must be spiritually connected, and we must be willing to take a stand. Nehemiah placed people on the wall, they took a stand. He told them not to be afraid. He told them that the Lord was with them. He reminded them of God's awesome power. Finally, he reminded them that they were standing on behalf of others.

When they took a stand that day they stood on behalf of their brothers. They didn't stand against their brothers, they stood for them. They took a stand that day for their children and their posterity. The benefits of their actions would be felt by those who would follow them. They were a community and they had to stand together.

Frequently we are asked to take stands of various kinds. Some times we stand for noble causes and the truths of Christ. However, all too often the stands we take are against our brothers. Many times we take stands against our children. If we will dare stand for Jesus together, as a united community, justice will indeed be restored.

We must learn to stand up. We must stand for those boys in prison. We must take a stand for our young people in public schools. We must fight for them. We must stand up for our sons and daughters. We must take them back from the dope dealers and pimps. We must take them back from the oppressor that has taught us to hate ourselves. We must stand up and proclaim that God does not make junk.

God loves us. If we love God, we must take a stand. We must stand for our posterity and our future. Deliverance comes as we take a stand. Paul wrote;

Galatians 5:1

It is for freedom that Christ has set us free. Stand firm, then, and do not let yourselves be burdened again by a yoke of slavery.

It is time for the church to take a stand. We must stand up for we have been sitting too long. We have been playing around too long. You ask, How are we going to stand when the dope dealers have all the money and they have drugs? How are we going to stand when there is so much wrong in our neighborhoods? You can stand because, if you look to heaven, you will find that Christ is standing for you.

The church is not to be some wimpish organization that submits to everyone and every idea that comes along. Jesus proclaimed that the church would be a militant force, not taking control through force, but winning the hearts of men to the truth. Once Jesus asked Simon Peter what others were saying about Him. He also asked Peter who he thought Jesus was. Peter answered that Jesus is the Christ, the Son of the Living God.

Matthew 16:17-19

Jesus replied, "Blessed are you, Simon son of Jonah, for this was not revealed to you by man, but by my Father in heaven. And I tell you that you are Peter, and on this rock I will build My church, and the gates of Hades will not overcome it. I will give you the keys of the kingdom of heaven; whatever you bind on earth will be bound in heaven, and whatever you loose on earth will be loosed in heaven."

The church is a powerful force in the world. We are the body of Christ to do His Will. Jesus said the very gates of Hell could not prevail against the church. We may think of the church as on the defensive, but this passage portrays the church as on the offensive. Our mission is to conquer the world with the truth of Christ even to the very gates of Hell. We will snatch souls from hells grasp through our work as warriors in God's Kingdom. We are not wimps. We are warriors out to conquer all that hell can throw at us!

Every time a believer stands for Christ, he is not standing alone. Jesus is there. If you take a stand, you will do so because God has stood up for you. He sees you as capable of making the stand. When the storms of life are raging, He will stand by us. When the world is tossing like a ship on the sea, the one who made both the winds and the sea will stand with us.

The cities seem dark and foreboding. It is indeed a dangerous place. However, there is a war taking place. It is a battle for the soul of black America. Oppressors have filled us with hate and vengeance. God wants to fill us with the power of love to do battle. As a people, our walls are down and we are vulnerable to the attacks of the enemy. However, there is hope.

From the ancient book of Nehemiah we have learned that there is a means of rebuilding and restoring our cities. God sent Nehemiah to rebuild Jerusalem. He will send us to rebuild our cities as well. We may be broken now, but God is raising up those who will be bold enough to take a stand.

The world is a broken place. It is shattered and scarred by sin, selfishness, and turmoil. However, God will give us strength to rebuild. He has a plan. He will cause His people to rise up with the right strategy and deliver His church from mediocrity and compromise. Although discouragement will come, He will allow us to have a mind to do the work and rebuild that which was broken. His Mighty Warriors will take a stand against the schemes of the enemy because nothing can hold back God's church.

Like Nehemiah, the people of our cities can rebuild the brokenness in their lives and communities once they have built a relationship with God and understand through Him all things are possible. God's power will remind the people that they not only have the compassion, but the courage to rebuild. The people can then respond, **"Let Us Rise Up and Rebuild."**

Review and Application

1. How do inner-conflicts hinder our progress?

2. Describe a wimpish mentality.

3. What is the importance of having a sense of family?

4. How does one become spiritually connected?